IRISH PUB CRACK

EILEEN BOYLE

Illustrated by James Campbell

THE
BLACKSTAFF PRESS

BELFAST

This book was written to record some of the crack that is part of everyday life in a small Irish pub. It is dedicated to the customers of the Castle Bar, who, without realising it, were providing the material collected here. May they continue for many a year to be as jovial and entertaining.

First published in 1997 by
The Blackstaff Press Limited
3 Galway Park, Dundonald, Belfast BT16 0AN, Northern Ireland

This edition prepared in 1998 for Irish Distillers Limited

© Introduction and compilation, Eileen Boyle, 1997
© Illustrations, James Campbell, 1997

Eileen Boyle has asserted her right under the Copyright, Designs and Patents
Act 1988 to be identified as the author of this work.

Typeset by Techniset Typesetters
Newton-le-Willows, Merseyside

Printed by The Guernsey Press Company Limited

A CIP catalogue record for this book
is available from the British Library

ISBN 0-85640-607-4

CONTENTS

'There is nothing which has yet been contrived
by man, by which so much happiness is
produced as by a good tavern or inn.'

SAMUEL JOHNSON

IN PRAISE OF
THE IRISH PUB

People say that television has killed the art of conversation. In some homes this may be true, but let me tell you, if the shenanigans in my bar any night of the week are anything to go by, conversation is alive and well. If a pub is to be a good breeding ground for conversation, what's needed is a civilised and lively atmosphere, and in ensuring that the mood is always congenial, bar staff can often have their work cut out for them. A good bartender will always have a ready supply of stimulating topics at hand to maintain a steady flow of crack and chatter. But the quality of the pub owes as much to its clientele as to its staff. And when a pub has plenty of character, and is filled with plenty of characters, it is the happiest place on earth.

What can be death to conversation, however, is a succession of boring monologues which nobody wants to hear. You can always find the punter who wants to hog the show; he doesn't want to converse at all, he just likes the sound of his own voice telling the assembled crew that he is right and they are wrong – recognise him? Happily, in an Irish pub nobody gets away with this game for long. The code is different here and the banter strong and the know-it-all is easily side-tracked. Perhaps some smart guy will gibe, 'Does your wife never let you talk at home?' – and the crack goes off in another direction.

In the bar over the years I've learned more about kindness and true Christianity than I ever have in any church – but then, I've also learned other things that I would never have heard about in any church either. The chitchat can be wonderful. There is so much give and take, the crack moves back and forth among the customers and they all get their chance to have their say. There are the naturally quiet ones who come to the pub and love to listen. And there are the star players who talk a lot and can bring out the wit and humour in others. At each gathering there's such a diversity of characters that the bar hums with entertainment and laughter.

Sometimes it's simply a matter of relaxing over a few jars, perhaps reading the newspaper which is always available, or talking quietly with some friends, background music playing, or maybe a game of draughts, or cards, or dominoes, or chess is under way. The mood may be jovial, with the exchange of yarns and jokes, or customers may start quizzing each other about any subject under the sun, though sport is invariably the favourite. And then there is the singsong, usually impromptu and utterly unsurpass-able. Anyone who can sing – and even some who can't

– will be coaxed into giving the company a rendering of their special party piece. After a few drinks inhibitions soon evaporate and many who might otherwise never dare to sing in public will find themselves on their feet with little prompting.

It has been said that the Irish plan their working life around their social life, and where's the harm in that? There are enough serious issues in life that cannot be avoided, so let's not make a serious business over our relaxation as well. Happiness is certainly the one goal each person pursues and the public house does its best to create the best climate to achieve that goal. I believe that the heart of the community lies within the walls of the pub, and if those walls could speak, what stories they would tell! Class is no barrier – doctor, teacher, labourer, retired or in work, all enjoy the crack. So let's love our neighbour by getting to know him – have a drink, a joke, a conversation with him and we'll not find it difficult, then, to like him. And the pub is the very place to do it.

EILEEN BOYLE, 1997
Castle Bar, Dromore

QUALITIES REQUIRED FOR A BARMAN

A good barman must be a diplomat, a democrat, an autocrat, an acrobat and a doormat. He must be capable of entertaining politicians, industrialists, the unemployed, pickpockets, gamblers, philanthropists, popsies and prudes. He must be on both sides of the political fence and be able to jump the fence. He should be, or should have been, a footballer, bowler, golfer, fisherman, tennis player, cricketer, darts player, pigeon fancier, racing driver, cyclist and linguist, as well as having a good knowledge of other sport involving dice, cards, horse racing and draughts. This is useful as he has sometimes to settle arguments and squabbles. He must be a qualified boxer, wrestler, weight lifter, sprinter and peacemaker.

He must always look immaculate when mixing with the ladies and the gentlemen mentioned above, as well as bankers, swankers, theatricals, commercial travellers, and company representatives, even though he has just made peace between any two, four or more of the forementioned patrons.

To be successful he must keep the bar full, the storeroom full, the wine cellar full, the customers full, but never get full himself. He must have staff who are clean, honest, quick workers, quick thinkers, non-drinkers, mathematicians, technicians, and at all times be on the boss's side, the customer's side, yet stay on the outside.

To sum up: he must be outside, inside, offside, dignified, sanctified, crucified, stupefied, cross-eyed, and if he's not the strong silent type, there's always suicide.

(Adapted from an original print, *c*. 1937)

THE THINGS THEY SAY
AMAZING FACTS AND FACTION

Over two thousand pints of beer are drunk in the House of Commons at Westminster each week.

A male seahorse is the only male creature that gives birth.

The River Nile froze over in the ninth and eleventh centuries.

A thick glass is more likely to crack than a thin glass if hot water is poured into it.

A man manufactures ten million new sperm cells in a day – enough in six months to populate the entire world.

Nearly half the people on earth live in one-thirteenth of the total land surface.

Estimated world population

1340	378 million
1600	498 million
1750	731 million
1900	1,668 million
1950	2,525 million
1980	4,360 million
1990	5,400 million

The United Nations estimates that by the year 2000 the world population will be 6,400 million.

The world's longest alphabet is Cambodian, with seventy-four letters. The shortest alphabet is Rotokas from the Soloman Islands, with eleven letters.

Charlemagne, 742–814 AD, king of the Franks and Holy Roman Emperor, couldn't read or write.

Augustus II of Saxony, elected king of Poland in 1697, had three hundred children, but his heir was his only legitimate son.

At Christmas 1969 black snow fell in Sweden.

A cow was once sentenced to two days in prison for eating the lawn outside the courthouse in Wellington, New Zealand.

Just before someone is struck by lightning their hair stands on end.

A newly born kangaroo is only half an inch long.

There are nearly four times as many insects in the world as the combined number of all other kinds of animal.

Leonardo da Vinci could simultaneously draw with one hand and write with the other.

An oyster can change sex several times during its life.

A newly born panda is about the size of a mouse.

On a still day in the Arctic you can hear a conversation taking place two miles away.

The song most frequently sung in the world is 'Happy Birthday to You'.

The British royal family's surname was chosen by a

commoner; originally it was Saxe-Coburg-Gotha, but in 1917, because of anti-German feeling, it was changed to Windsor, the name being selected by a private secretary to George v.

The nail of your middle finger grows the fastest, the thumbnail the slowest.

In England in 1338 there was non-stop rain from June until December.

A female black widow spider eats the male after mating.

A shark lays the largest eggs in the world.

If the global harvest was shared out equally, there would be 5lbs of food per day for each person.

In 1914 a display was held to mark the completion of the Panama Canal; an invitation was sent officially to a non-existent organisation – the Swiss Navy. An embarrassed US State Department later gave an order to withdraw the invitation.

The Panama Canal is the only place in the world from which you can watch the sun rise over the Pacific Ocean and set over the Atlantic.

The Great Wall of China is visible from outer space.

Snails can sleep, without wakening, for years at a time.

In 1979 snow fell on the Sahara Desert.

The coastline of Alaska is longer than the combined coastlines of all other American states.

THE JOKER

It is very seldom that ecclesiastical top dogs visit the parish, so one day when the archbishop came, a press conference was held, and Joe, the local reporter, desperately wanted a scoop.

He managed to get in with the first question. 'Will you be visiting the red light district?'

The archbishop, really taken aback, said, 'Is there a red light district in this town?'

The newspaper had its headline: ARCHBISHOP'S FIRST WORDS ARE: IS THERE A RED LIGHT DISTRICT IN THIS TOWN?

The old gent was backing his Rolls into the last parking space when a zippy sports car whipped in behind him to beat him to it.

The young man jumped out and said, 'Sorry, Pops, but you've got to be young and smart to do that.'

The old man ignored the remark and kept reversing until the Rolls had smashed the sports car into a crumpled heap. 'Sorry, son, but you've got to be old and rich to do that.'

There was an argument going on about which was the oldest profession.

The surgeon rose to his feet and said: 'When God created Eve he took a rib from Adam in the first surgical operation.'

The architect made his claim: 'In order to restore order from chaos, God must have needed the services of an architect.'

The civil servant came in with the clincher: 'Ah, but who created chaos?'

There were two signs outside the Pearly Gates. A long queue of men lined up at the first sign which read: HENPECKED HUSBANDS REPORT HERE.

Only one small timid man stood at the second sign which read: LIBERATED MEN REPORT HERE.

Saint Peter asked him, 'Why are you standing here?'

He answered, 'Because the wife told me to.'

When the doctor rang the plumber about a fault that had developed in the toilet cistern, the plumber reminded him that it was 3.00 a.m.

'So what?' said the doctor. 'I get called out in the middle of the night as well.'

Ten minutes later the plumber arrived and was shown to the bathroom. He lifted the lid off the cistern and popped in two aspirins. Then he flushed the toilet. 'If it hasn't improved by the morning, ring me again,' he said.

Several clergymen arrived together at the Pearly Gates. While they waited, the trumpets sounded and a further arrival came and was ushered straight in. The clergymen were amazed and asked Saint Peter the reason why.

Saint Peter told them: 'That was a taxman and during his lifetime on earth he has put the fear of God into more people than the whole lot of you put together.'

This middle-aged couple had played golf together for all their married life. One day they were sitting in front of the fire chatting to each other when the wife asked, 'If I die before you, will you get married again?'

The husband looked at her and muttered, 'I suppose so.'

'Would you play golf with her?' was the next question.

'Oh, I guess so,' he muttered again.

'Would you let her use my golf clubs?' the wife enquired.

'Oh no,' he said, 'she's got her own. She uses left-handed clubs.'

When the local council decided to build a fountain in the town they put the project out to tender. They received quotes from three contractors – Castle Building, Bridge Construction, and Fixall.

The town clerk interviewed the Castle Building manager and his price was £3,000.

'Would you please break that down?' requested the clerk.

'It's £1,000 for materials, £1,000 for wages and £1,000 for us,' replied the manager.

Then the Bridge Construction manager was interviewed and he quoted: '£6,000 – £2,000 for wages, £2,000 for materials and £2,000 for us.'

Lastly, Seán went to tender for Fixall. He quoted £9,000 and assured the clerk that his firm was definitely the best for the job. When asked to break down the price, he said, '£3,000 for materials, £3,000 for us and £3,000 for Castle Building to do the job.'

In the pub one evening Trevor was telling his friend Nigel, 'I had an operation and the surgeon left a bit of sponge in me.'

'That's terrible,' Nigel sympathised. 'Have you got any pain?'

'No,' said Trevor, 'but I've an awful thirst.'

In the bar the conversation went as follows: 'Wasn't it tough luck on Davy. He missed two maintenance payments and the wife repossessed him.'

A man, a little the worse for drink, leaned over and offered the lady sitting beside him a double whiskey and soda. She was affronted but managed to swallow the insult.

'Are you a gardening expert?' a little girl asked the woman who lived next door.

'No, dear, indeed I am not. Why do you ask that?' said the woman.

'Well, Mum and Dad were talking and Dad said if there's any dirt to be dug up you're the one to do it.'

Billy, an Englishman who had come to live in the town, was speaking to Kieran in the bar.

'Have you lived here all your life?' he asked.

'Oh, I hope not yet,' he was told.

Barmaid on the phone: 'You'll have to give me a better description than that. The pub is full of drunken layabouts who should have been home hours ago.'

'Your glass is empty – will you have another one?' asked Stephen.

'Now why would I be wanting two empty glasses?' asked Johnny.

The husband of a customer had died; she had five young children to rear so it was decided to raise money in the bar to help her. When Jim and Patsy came in for a drink the barman served them and then asked if they would like a ticket in the raffle.

'What's it for?' asked Patsy.

'Jane Cunningham and her five children,' the barman told him.

Patsy shook his head. 'I'm too old to take on that many at my time of day.'

The train was rattling towards a long tunnel and in one carriage sat an Englishman, an Irishman, a pretty young woman and an old lady. The train entered the tunnel and everything went dark. There was a loud kiss followed at once by an even louder smack. When the train emerged from the tunnel the four passengers were all in their seats, preoccupied with their thoughts.

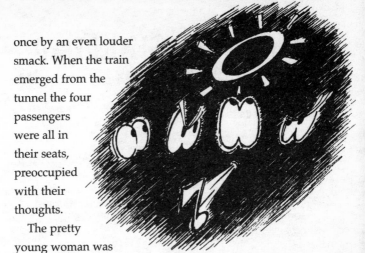

The pretty young woman was thinking: 'Why should that Irishman want to kiss an old lady?'

The old lady was thinking: 'That young hussy sitting there as though nothing had happened when that Englishman is just after kissing her!'

The Englishman was thinking: 'Why should I get my face slapped when I didn't do a damned thing?'

The Irishman was thinking: 'How about that! I make a kissing sound and then smack an Englishman right on the mouth and get away with it!'

Raymond, a gentleman getting on in years, was sitting at the bar crying. 'I got married to a lovely young divorcée last week. She's a great cook, makes sure I take my vitamins and garlic and keeps my clothes in great nick for me.'

'Then why are you crying?' asked Will.

'Because I can't remember where we live,' sobbed Raymond.

BAFFLED AND BEWILDERED

Answers on page 85

1 Use eight 8s to make 1,000.

2 GUINNESS IS GOOD FOR YOU
Read this aloud. Read again. Slower this time. Now, one last time. Say aloud the first letter of each word.

3 Have an unopened Hennessy brandy bottle. Request someone to drink a halfun from the bottle without breaking the seal or the bottle.

4 l0 l0 l0
With just one stroke to the above, make 950.

5 Three men went to a hotel and were told there was only one room free. It would cost them £30 for the night. They paid £10 each. The receptionist discovered by mistake that she had overcharged them by £5 and asked the porter to return the £5. He gave each of the three men £1 and kept the other £2 himself. Each man had actually paid £9 – a total of £27 for the room. Add to that the £2 the porter kept and that is £29. What happened to the other £1?

6 Nine dots:
   •   •   •
   •   •   •
   •   •   •

Connect these dots, without lifting the pen, using four straight lines.

7 Make a sentence by rearranging the following:
0 0 0 0 1 1 2 4 8

8 A glass of whiskey and a glass of water: can you mix the two, keeping the water at the bottom of the glass and the whiskey sitting at the top?

9 Have a pen and a piece of paper.
   A man went into a chip shop and he asked for two fish.
   The waitress wrote down: 2F
   Then a pie and peas. She wrote: PP
   Then a pastie and chips. She wrote: PC
   And a sausage supper. She wrote: SS
   Looking up at the man, she said, 'You're from the
   Salvation Army.'
   How did she know? Hand the piece of paper to
   the person being asked.

10 How many triangles can you find in this figure?

11 There are nine wolves in a square enclosure at the
   zoo. Build two more square enclosures and put
   each wolf in a pen by itself.

12 You have ten horses and nine single horse boxes. Can
   you put the ten horses in the box without doubling up?

13 5 + 5 + 5 = 550
   By using only one stroke make this correct.

14 Draw this without lifting your pencil:

15 Which letter is missing from the following:
   B D F H J N P V

16 Each son in the Jones family has as many brothers as
   one-quarter the total number of children. Each daughter
   has twice as many sisters as she has brothers. How
   many boys and girls are there in the Jones family?

17 A man lived on the eighth floor in a block of flats. Each morning he took the lift down to the ground floor and went off to his work. Coming home in the evening, he took the lift to the third floor and walked the remaining five. Why?

18 A man is given nineteen saplings. He wants to plant them in nine rows with five trees in each row. How does he do it? Draw out the plan on paper.

19 H I J K L M N O
That is your clue. The answer is a common word with five letters.

20 You have three empty glasses in a row with three full ones beside them. How can you move the glasses so that the full and empty glasses alternate? You are allowed three moves and each time you must pick up two glasses that are beside one another.

21 O T T F F S S E _ _
Give the next two letters.

22 Take a cigarette and ask someone to join the top of the cigarette to the bottom without breaking it.

23 Plant ten trees in five rows with four trees in each row.

24 A farmer had eleven cows and he wanted to divide them between his three sons. He wanted to give $\frac{1}{2}$ to the first son, $\frac{1}{4}$ to the second, and one-sixth to the third. He wanted to be fair and cause no jealousy or arguments among them. How could he divide the animals?

25 G E G S (9, 4)
    What is the answer to this crossword clue?

26 Last week I spent half the money I had in my piggy
    bank. This means I am now left with as many pence as I
    had pounds before and half as many pounds as I had
    pence. How much money did I start off with?

27 Use x, +, −, ÷, decimal point, square root signs or
    brackets to make:
    1 1 1 = 3
    2 2 2 = 3
    3 3 3 = 3
    4 4 4 = 3
    5 5 5 = 3
    6 6 6 = 3
    7 7 7 = 3
    8 8 8 = 3
    9 9 9 = 3

28 Arrange the numbers 1 to 7 so that, when added, they
    will equal 100.

29 Get an empty wine bottle and push the cork right down
    into it. Ask someone to remove the cork without
    breaking the bottle.

30 Put three glasses in a row on the table, with the middle
    one upright and the outside ones
    upside-down. Request someone to turn them all the
    right way up in three moves, turning two glasses each
    time. First
    demonstrate it to
    your volunteer like
    this:

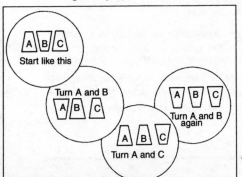

Start like this

Turn A and B

Turn A and B
again

Turn A and C

Now turn glass B
upside down and
challenge someone
else to do it.

31 How many triangles are there in this figure?

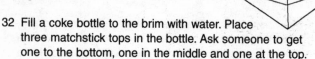

32 Fill a coke bottle to the brim with water. Place three matchstick tops in the bottle. Ask someone to get one to the bottom, one in the middle and one at the top.

33 An aeroplane flies due North for 800 miles. The same aeroplane then flies due South for 800 miles. The same aeroplane is then 1,600 miles from where it took off. How?

34 There is a man, a fox, a hen and a bag of corn on one side of a river. The man needs to cross the river but he can only carry one thing at a time. If he leaves the hen and corn alone, the hen will eat the corn. If he leaves the hen and the fox alone, the fox will eat the hen. How does he cross?

35 An old miser saves all the stubs of the candles he has burnt. From every nine stubs he can make a candle. If the miser has 345 stubs, what is the highest number of candles he can possibly make?

36 Place a whiskey glass upside down on a plate containing water. Ask someone to get the water in the glass without touching the plate.

37 Draw the following without lifting your pen.

38 Ten sheep are kept in a circular pen. Make three more circular pens and put each sheep in a pen by itself.

39 A spy was easily captured because his message was so simple to decode. What does it say? Alice: Tom told Ann, Carter, Kelly and Ted, David Atwood was not moving out now. David awaiting you.

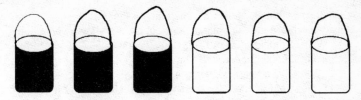

40 You have three full buckets of milk and three empty
    ones. By moving only one bucket, line them up so that
    the full and empty buckets alternate.

41 A wine merchant dies leaving his three sons seven
    barrels full of wine, seven barrels half full and seven
    empty barrels. In his will he specifies that each son will
    receive exactly the same number of full, half full and
    empty barrels. How can his wish be granted?

42 Divide this figure into four equal parts of
    the same size and shape.

43 A woman buys 100 toys for £100.
    Toys A are £10 each.
    Toys B are £3 each.
    Toys C are 50p each.
    How many of each did she buy?

44 A bus company does not allow passengers to carry
    luggage over 4 feet long onto its buses. A man has a
    fishing rod 5 feet long. How can he take it onto the bus?

45 Without lifting your pen from the paper join all sixteen
    dots with six straight lines.

        •   •   •   •
        •   •   •   •
        •   •   •   •
        •   •   •   •

46 Here are the scrambled letters of an everyday object. Unscramble the word.
R R R R F G I A E E O T

47 How many 9s do you pass when you start at 1 and work your way up to 100?

48 Divide this figure into four equal parts of the same shape and size.

49 While Jack was walking his dog he met his mother-in-law's only daughter's son. What relation was this person to Jack?

THE PIG GOT UP AND SLOWLY WALKED AWAY

One evening in October, when I was one-third sober,
And taking home a load with manly pride,
My poor feet began to stutter, so I lay down in the gutter,
And a pig came up and lay down by my side.
Then we sang, 'It's all fair weather when good fellows get
    together',
Till a lady passing by was heard to say,
'You can tell a man who boozes from the company he
    chooses',
And the pig got up and slowly walked away.

I also well remember an evening in November
When I was creeping home at break of day,
For in my exhilaration I engaged in conversation
With a cab horse on the corner of Broadway.
I was filled up to the eyeballs with a flock of gin and
    highballs.
So I whispered to the cab horse old and grey:
'It's these all-night homeward marches that give us both
    our fallen arches',
And the cab horse laughed and slowly walked away.

NOW YOU'RE TALKING!

Drink. Get drunk.

When drunk, fall asleep.

If asleep, you can commit no sin.

When you commit no sin you go to heaven.

So, let's all drink

And go to heaven.

If you want to be heard, SHOUT.
If you want to be seen, STAND.
If you want to be appreciated, SHUT UP!

When God made man
The whole world rested.
When God made woman
Neither God nor man rested.

Women have many faults,
Men have only two:
Everything they say
And everything they do.

Don't question your wife's choice.
Look who she married.

LIES, DAMNED LIES AND STATISTICS

You can prove virtually anything you want using statistics. Governments do it all the time, large corporations do it and very ordinary people enjoying a very ordinary conversation do it regularly. Throwaway lines get used when actual figures are not available.

Ten per cent of road accidents are caused by people who have been drinking. I've heard this recounted in the bar as: 'People with no drink are nine times more likely to be involved in a road accident as the man with a drink or two.'

As a marriage consists of a man and woman getting married (or did until recently), it is logical to say that half the people who get married are men. Let this come up with an argumentative crowd and it will turn out that half the men are gay and the other half get married. Or perhaps only half the number of men who get married want to!

Statistics prove that beds can cause headaches or upset stomachs. People can go out drinking and maybe go home drunk, but happy as the day is long. They'll go to bed and wake up in the morning with a splitting headache or sore guts – so it must have been the bed that was the cause.

The following unusual table deals with statistics relating to the six main leaders during the Second

World War (1939–1945). Could they mean that God was on the side of the Allies?

Taking the second column as an example, this is how the table works: the UK leader, Winston Churchill, was born in 1874; he came to power in 1940 when he replaced Neville Chamberlain as prime minister, and he had been in power for five years when the war ended in 1945; he was by then aged seventy-one. It is interesting that even though each ruler was born in a different year, the sum total of the statistics for each of their lives comes to 3,890. If this figure is then divided by two, it works out at 1945, the very year that the war ended. However, it is even more surprising to find that if you take the first letter of each of the rulers' names (C, S, R, I, H, T) and rearrange them, the six letters spell out the name CHRIST. Strange, but true!

The Rulers	Churchill	Stalin	Roosevelt	*Il Duce	Hitler	*Tito
Country	UK	USSR	USA	Italy	Germany	Yugoslavia
Year of Birth	1874	1879	1882	1883	1889	1892
Age in 1945	71	66	63	62	56	53
Gained Power	1940	1922	1933	1922	1933	1941
No. of years in power by 1945	5	23	12	23	12	4
Total	3890	3890	3890	3890	3890	3890
Divide by 2	1945	1945	1945	1945	1945	1945

*Il Duce's proper name was Benito Mussolini; Tito's was Josip Broz.

THE LONG LOST ARM OF COINCIDENCE

An American group has been looking into the phenomenon of 'history repeating itself'. It comes up with the following amazing coincidences:

Both President Kennedy and President Lincoln were concerned with civil rights. Lincoln was elected in 1860, Kennedy in 1960. Both had children die during their presidencies. Both were killed on a Friday in front of their wives. Both were shot in the head from behind.

Their successors, both named Johnston, were southern Democrats, and both were in the Senate. Andrew Johnston was born in 1808; Lyndon Johnston was born in 1908.

John Wilkes Booth – Lincoln's killer – was born in 1839; Lee Harvey Oswald – Kennedy's killer – in 1939. Both were southerners favouring unpopular ideas. Both were assassinated before trial.

Lincoln's secretary, whose name was Kennedy, advised him not to go to the theatre. Kennedy's secretary, whose name was Lincoln, advised him not to go to Dallas.

John Wilkes Booth shot Lincoln in a theatre and ran to a warehouse.

Lee Harvey Oswald shot Kennedy from a warehouse and ran to a theatre.

TALL TALES – TRUTH OR MYTH?

Late one night Sally was driving home, having been to visit her parents in a nearby town. It was a horrible dark night, with sleety rain and a high wind, and as she was driving along she saw a woman standing at a bus stop, trying to hold up an umbrella. Sally felt sorry for her and decided to give her a lift – at least part of the way home. So she pulled over, and the soaking woman got into the car.

Sally noticed that she was a big woman, with coarse features and very badly applied make-up. She tried to talk to her but with no success. Then she noticed that the woman's hands, holding her handbag, were very large and hairy.

By this time Sally was feeling very uncomfortable so she said to her passenger: 'Would you mind getting out and checking my back lights. Two cars have passed and flashed their lights and I'm afraid mine might not be working.'

Sally stopped her car at the side of the road and the strange woman got out. Quickly, Sally slammed the door shut and drove off as fast as she could to the nearest police station. As she drew to a halt she saw that the woman's handbag was still lying on the passenger seat. She took it into the station, handed it to the policeman and then related her story to him. The policeman inspected the bag for clues.

'Looks like you've had a very lucky escape,' he said, as he drew out of the bag a blood-stained hatchet.

PADDY THE IRISHMAN

One time Paddy went to visit his sister in England and he called into a local pub for a pint. He chatted to all the customers, as he would at home, but they simply looked at him, obviously not wishing to be involved in conversation with him.

A man standing beside Paddy was wearing a lot of expensive jewellery.

'That's a beautiful ring you're wearing,' said Paddy.

'Oh, that's more than a ring,' answered the man. 'If I twist the ring clockwise I get a direct line to the Prime Minister in London.'

'You're wearing a gorgeous bracelet too,' said Paddy.

'Yes,' said the Englishman, 'it is something special as well. When I twist it anticlockwise I have a hot line to the President of America.'

Paddy went to the toilet at this stage and when he returned there was toilet paper sticking out of his trouser pocket. In a sneering tone the Englishman told Paddy he was carrying the toilet paper with him.

'Not at all,' said Paddy. 'That's a fax I've just received from the pope.'

Paddy the Irishman, Paddy the Englishman and Paddy the Scotsman were sentenced to be hanged together but were given the choice of tree from which they were to hang.

Paddy the Englishman said he wished to be hanged from an old English oak. The Scotsman chose a Scots fir, but Paddy the Irishman said he wanted to hang from a gooseberry bush. The judge agreed to the first two but told Paddy the Irishman that a gooseberry bush was neither big enough nor strong enough.

'Don't worry, yer Honour, I can wait till it grows,' Paddy said.

Paddy won £8 million on the National Lottery and he went over to London to collect his winnings. They were short of cash and wrote a cheque for £4 million, requesting him to return in a month for the remaining £4 million.

Paddy got angry. 'If you're going to mess me about like this just keep your auld lottery and give me back my pound,' he said.

Two Englishmen were making counterfeit £20 notes but the machine developed a fault and printed them out as £18 notes.

'What are we going to do with these?' says one.

'No hassle,' replied the other. 'We'll bring them to Ireland and get rid of them there.'

So when they arrived in Ireland they went into a pub and asked the barman would he change the notes.

'No problem,' says the barman. 'Would you like three £6 notes or two £9 notes?'

Paddy and his friend went to a pub. They were talking away, when Paddy called the publican over and asked him to settle an argument.

'Are there two pints or four pints in a quart?' asked Paddy.

'There are two pints in a quart,' confirmed the publican.

Then the two men moved along the bar and Paddy said to the barmaid, 'Two pints of ale, please, and they're on the house.'

When the barmaid showed grave doubt, Paddy shouted up to the publican, 'You did say two pints, didn't you?'

'That's right,' said the publican. 'Two pints.'

A particularly unpopular sergeant-major popped his head up above the trench and a sniper's bullet whizzed past his ear.

'Paddy, get that sniper,' he roared out.

Within ten minutes Paddy returned with the enemy sniper – hands raised above his head. Then Paddy began to punch the devil out of him.

'Hey, go easy. What's that for?' asked one of his mates.

'It's for missing the bloody sergeant-major,' said Paddy.

A ventriloquist with his dummy on his lap was making several offensive jokes at the expense of the Irish.

Paddy could take it no longer, so he shouted, 'Hey, I object to your making fun of my countrymen.'

'I'm sorry,' said the ventriloquist. 'I meant no offence.'

'Oh, it's not you,' said Paddy. 'It's that cheeky little bastard on your lap.'

Paddy went into the pub and the publican said to him, 'Good evening, sir, would you like a drink?'

'Yes,' said Paddy. 'I'll have a double Bush and a pint of Guinness.'

The drinks were placed in front of him and the publican said, '£4.35, please.'

'No,' said Paddy, 'it's your treat. You asked me would I like a drink.'

Another customer at the bar said, 'He's right, you know. I'm a solicitor and I distinctly heard you ask him to have a drink.'

The angry publican told Paddy to drink his drink,

then leave and never come back.

Ten minutes later Paddy returned.

'I thought I told you never to come back,' roared the publican.

Paddy insisted he had never been there before in his life.

The publican remarked, 'Well, you must have a double!'

'Thanks very much,' said Paddy. 'And one for my solicitor friend across the bar as well.'

P addy was in London and he went into a pub and ordered a double whiskey. 'Will an Irish tenner be all right?' he asked.

'No problem,' said the barman.

So Paddy, in his lovely tenor voice, broke into 'The Londonderry Air'.

P addy ordered a pint of Guinness but as soon as it was placed in front of him he cancelled the order and requested a pint of Bass instead. When he had drunk it the barman asked for the money.

Paddy got indignant. 'I gave you a pint of Guinness for it.'

'But you hadn't paid for that either,' said the barman.

'Well, why should I? I didn't drink it, sure I didn't?' said Paddy.

Paddy went into the bar and said to the barman, 'Drinks all round, please, and take one yourself.'

Paddy was immediately the toast of the bar. Then the barman requested the money.

'But I haven't got a penny,' said Paddy.

The barman grabbed him by the neck and hurled him out of the pub.

A few minutes later Paddy came back into the bar. 'Drinks all round,' he declared. 'But not for you, barman. One drink and you go bloody mad.'

Paddy had been a barman in the same pub for thirty years without ever going on holiday.

'Why don't you travel and broaden your mind,' he was repeatedly told.

Finally he took their advice and went for a holiday to the Canary Islands. When he returned he was a changed and knowledgeable man.

'Well, what did you learn?' asked the regulars.

'I can tell you this,' said Paddy, 'there are no canaries on the Canary Islands.'

A year passed and the regulars suggested to Paddy he should try the Virgin Islands this time.

When Paddy returned he was asked: 'What did you learn on this holiday?'

'I can tell you this,' said Paddy as they all leaned forward to hear, 'there are no canaries on the Virgin Islands either.'

The solicitor told Paddy that if he wanted to be defended in court the following day he would need money. But Paddy was almost broke.

'All I've got is an antique gold watch,' he said.

'Well,' said the solicitor, 'that's OK, you can make

some money on that. Now, what are you accused of stealing?'

'An antique gold watch,' said Paddy.

The funeral of a very rich man was taking place and Paddy joined the mourners. He wailed and moaned and cried louder than any of them. Everybody was looking at him, wondering who he was and trying to comfort him.

One of the dead man's relatives said to Paddy, 'We didn't realise you knew him so well.'

'That's the trouble,' said Paddy, 'I didn't.'

Paddy and his friend went fishing one Sunday morning. As they happily sat on the bank of the river, they heard the church bells ring in the distance.

Paddy's friend said sorrowfully, 'You know, we really ought to be in church.'

Busily baiting his hook, Paddy replied, 'I couldn't have gone today anyhow – my wife is very ill in bed.'

Paddy walked into the pub and his mates at the bar started sniggering.

'What's up with you all?' says Paddy.

'You left your bedroom blind up last night and the lights were on. That was some show you and the missus put on,' said one of his mates.

'Well, that's where you're wrong. Don't take me for a fool. I wasn't even home last night.'

Paddy the Irishman, Paddy the Englishman and Paddy the Scotsman were lost in a desert. They were hot, thirsty, tired and thoroughly fed up when they

came across a genie's lamp. Paddy the Englishman rubbed it and the genie came out.

'You may have one wish granted. What is your wish?'

The Englishman wished he was back in England and he disappeared. Paddy the Scotsman then rubbed the lamp and again the genie emerged to give him his wish. The Scotsman wanted to get back to Scotland – and immediately he disappeared.

Paddy the Irishman then decided to rub the lamp and once again the genie came out to grant him his wish.

'Oh, I'm all alone here!' said Paddy the Irishman. 'Can I have my friends, the Englishman and the Scotsman, back, please?'

Paddy had been stranded on a desert island for two years, when one day he saw a lifeboat drifting close enough for him to swim to it. Paddy dragged the lifeboat to the beach, took it apart, and built himself a raft with the pieces.

Paddy the Irishman was intent on saving the man on the edge of the cliff.

'Don't jump,' he said. 'Think of your wife and kids.'

'I have no wife and kids,' the man said.

'Then think of your mother and father,' said Paddy.

'I have no mother or father,' said the man.

'Then think of Saint Patrick,' said Paddy.

'Who is Saint Patrick?' asked the man.

'Ach! Jump ye bloody heathen,' said Paddy.

Paddy phoned the fire brigade.

'Quick, there's a fire! There's a fire!' said Paddy.

'Where is it?' asked the voice at the other end of the line.

'In my place, of course,' said Paddy.

'I mean, what's the location?'

'It's in the kitchen. Hurry,' said Paddy.

'But how do we get there?'

'My God! Haven't you got a fire engine?'

Paddy the Irishman, Paddy the Englishman and Paddy the Scotsman were all due to be executed. They were to be shot by a firing squad.

Paddy the Englishman was first and as he stood waiting to be shot he shouted, 'FLOOD!' The execution squad all ran away.

Paddy the Scotsman's turn came and as he waited he shouted, 'EARTHQUAKE!' and again the execution squad ran.

Then came Paddy the Irishman's turn. Thinking he'd got the hang of this, he shouted 'FIRE!' so they all drew their guns and fired.

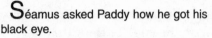

Séamus asked Paddy how he got his black eye.

'You'll never believe this,' said Paddy, 'but I got it in church.'

He told Séamus he had been sitting behind a fat lady in church. When they stood up for a hymn he noticed that her dress was tucked into the cheeks of her bum.

'All I did was bend forward and pull it out,' said Paddy. 'But she turned round and hit me.'

A week later Paddy had another black eye.

'I was sitting behind the same fat woman in church and when we stood up for a hymn her dress was tucked into the cheeks of her bum again. My little nephew leaned forward and pulled it out, but I knew she didn't like that, so I leaned forward to push it back in.'

Paddy went to the doctor for his annual check-up.

'Your hearing is getting worse,' said the doctor. 'And you'll have to cut out drinking, smoking and sex.'

'What?' cried Paddy. 'Just so I can hear better?'

An Englishman boarded a train with a large shaggy dog and he sat opposite Paddy.

Paddy looked long and hard at the dog and then said, 'And what type of dog would that be?'

The Englishman replied, 'It's a cross between an ape and an Irishman.'

Paddy quickly responded, 'You mean it's related to the both of us.'

Paddy cleaned out the bookies on the day of the Grand National. His friends were soon pressing him to divulge his system.

'I'm superstitious and I watch out for omens,' said Paddy. 'On my way to the races I took a number 8 bus. It stopped 8 times on the way and it cost me £8 to get into the track. Now that was three 8s telling me something. Well, three 8s are 21, so I backed number 21.'

The owner of the corner shop was adamant. She told Paddy, 'I'm sorry, but you can have no more credit. Your bill is already bigger than it should be.'

'I know that,' retorted Paddy. 'As soon as you cut it down to the proper amount, I'll pay it.'

'Hey, Billy, lend me £20 till pay day to buy a round of drinks,' said Paddy.

Billy thought for a minute and then said, 'OK, but when is pay day?'

'How would I know?' said Paddy. 'Sure you're the one who's working.'

Paddy, his wife and seven children were returning from a shopping spree and as they stood at the bus stop a blind man joined them. When the bus arrived it was almost full and had room for only eight people.

'OK, love,' said Paddy to his wife, 'you go ahead with the children. The two of us will walk.'

The blind man had little option but to walk with Paddy, but after a while the tap, tap, tap of his stick started to annoy Paddy.

'That tap, tap, tap is driving me crazy,' said Paddy. 'Can't you put a piece of rubber on the end of it?'

The blind man made a quick response: 'If you had put a bit of rubber on the end of your own stick, there'd have been room for us on the bus.'

Paddy was coming through customs at the airport, carrying a large parcel.

'What have you got there?' asked the suspicious customs officer.

'It's Lourdes holy water,' said Paddy. 'My mother has had pains so I got it for her.'

The officer unwrapped the parcel and inside was a bottle which he opened and tasted. 'It's whiskey!' he spluttered.

'Lord bless me,' said Paddy. 'Another bloody miracle.'

Paddy the Irishman, Paddy the Englishman, and Paddy the Scotsman had all been given the death sentence. They were to have their heads chopped off. On the day of the beheadings they were given the choice of facing up, or down, on the guillotine.

Paddy the Englishman was first and he chose to face downwards. When the rope was pulled the blade fell halfway, then stopped.

The authorities were shocked and said, 'It's a miracle! He must be released immediately!'

The Englishman was released and Paddy the Scotsman was led to the guillotine. He also chose to face downwards. The rope was pulled, but again the blade stopped halfway. The authorities were very alarmed this time, and ordered his immediate release.

Next, Paddy the Irishman was led up to the guillotine and he chose to face upwards. The rope was pulled and for the third time the blade stopped halfway.

The authorities said: 'We cannot understand this. He must also be released!'

But Paddy the Irishman suddenly shouted: 'Wait! I can explain. There's a piece of wood there that's making the blade stick.'

THINK TANK

Answers on page 89

1 The perfect man, the perfect woman and Santa Claus
were in a lift together. On the floor lay a £10 note. Who
picked it up?

2 What is the definition of a bachelor?

3 What's the best way to increase the size of your bank
balance?

4 How did Bolton Wanderers win the FA Challenge Cup
and never score a goal?

5 What is the only Scottish team that plays on Irish soil for
home games?

6 If you had only one match and went into a room in
which there was an oil lamp, a log fire and a stove,
which would you light first?

7 Can a man living in Northern Ireland be buried in the
Republic of Ireland?

8 Is it legal in Northern Ireland for a man to marry his
widow's sister?

9 Is there a Twelfth of July in the Republic of Ireland?

10 Imagine you are the captain of a ship. The ship sails at
50 miles per hour and travels 40 miles North, 30 miles
East and 290 miles South. What age is the captain?

11 Water lilies double in area every twenty-four hours. At
the beginning of the summer there is one water lily on a
pond. It takes sixty days for the lake to be completely
covered. On what day is it half covered?

12 Two men play chess. They played five games each and won the same number of games. How?

13 A woman goes into a hardware shop to buy something for her house. She asks the price and is told that 1 costs £1. The price of 30 is £2 and 144 costs £3. What does she want to buy?

14 A smart explorer is captured by savages who tell him: 'Make a statement. If what you say is true, you will be hanged. If it is false you will be shot.' How can he save his life?

15 What can a white hen do that a black hen can't?

16 Can you mention a five-letter word that is pronounced the same when four letters are removed?

17 If a plane crashes on the border of Northern Ireland and the Republic of Ireland, where are the survivors buried?

18 How many animals of each species did Moses take onto the ark?

19 How many months of the year have twenty-eight days?

20 Write down the word S C O T L A N D.
Get the name of footballer for each letter who played in a number 7 jersey.

21 An electric train heads north at 80 miles per hour. The wind is blowing from the east at 20 miles per hour. In what direction will the smoke go?

22 Nine golf balls are placed this:

o o o
o o o
o o o

Connect them using three straight lines.

23 Can you find a word with only one vowel that is repeated six times?

24 Can you find a word with only one consonant?

25 Can you find a word with six consonants in a row?

26 Can you find a word containing all the vowels in the correct order?

27 Find the product of (x - a)(x - b)(x - c) etc., to (x - z).

AN ULSTERMAN'S LETTER TO THE DHSS

Dear Sir,

In respect of receiving the AIDS leaflet through my door, I would like to apply straightaway for AIDS.

I have been on the dole for the past ten years and I have been on supplementary benefit and every other state benefit I could get. It now seems I will be getting state aid for sex. It's a pity AIDS has come so late as I already have fifteen children. I wonder will you be making any back payments?

Your letter states that the more sex I have, the more chance I have of getting AIDS. My biggest problem here is persuading my wife who is not so keen after fifteen children. Several years ago I bought some aids but she showed little interest and they were hardly used. Would there be any chance of a refund for the £17.80 I paid for these gadgets?

Anyway, I will now explain to her that the Government will be paying for all the sex we have. We can't let a chance like this slip by.

You also state that I can pass my AIDS on but you will understand that with a wife and fifteen children to feed there won't be much left to pass on. If by any chance there is a bit, I will pass it on to my poor old mother-in-law.

I understand from your letter that I can get AIDS from a blood transfusion, and I intend writing to my local hospital to see when I can get one. Will the AIDS I get from the hospital be deducted from the AIDS I get from you? Perhaps you will write and let me know.

I am a firm believer in getting every aid from the country I can get, and I'm sure you will agree that by my recent performances I do qualify for this one.

Could you let me know how much I will get each time and will it be weekly or monthly payments?

PS Your advert is great. I certainly won't die of ignorance. I know my rights.

MORE AMAZING
FACTS AND FACTION

Twenty-six countries in the world have no coastline.

A bottle of alcohol now marked % pure alcohol used to be marked proof – 35 per cent was 70 proof. The alcohol was 'proved' by pouring it into gunpowder and igniting it; if it burnt evenly it was 50 per cent pure alcohol and was deemed 100 proof.

With an area of around one million square miles Arabia is the largest peninsula in the world.

When archaeologists were digging under the Leaning Tower of Pisa in 1992, they discovered an ancient Roman house less than three feet below ground.

James Scott of Brisbane, Australia, was lost in a blizzard in the Himalayas but he survived for forty-three days on only two chocolate bars.

There are thirty mass killings annually in the USA. One-quarter of US schools have shooting incidents each year.

Water pipes underground will often freeze during a warm spell that follows a cold snap. The explanation is that after a cold spell a large quantity of heat is taken from the ground in the work of changing the frozen moisture into water and this, on the principle of the ice cream in the freezer, the pipe is chilled – enough heat being taken from it to freeze it.

Saint John was the only member of the twelve apostles to die a natural death.

Dogs sweat through their paws and nose.

The ancestry of every thoroughbred horse in the world can be traced to one of three Arabian stallions imported to England in the eighteenth century.

You use three times as many muscles to frown as you do to smile.

South Africa's Kruger National Park is home to an elephant who thinks he's a buffalo. In the early 1970s five baby elephants were released in the park close to a herd of buffalo. One elephant joined the herd and adopted the habits of the buffalo. In 1980 a park visitor saw the ten-year-old elephant, with twenty buffalo, trumpeting and bellowing to drive eight lions away from a waterhole. He has also been seen running away, like the rest of the buffalo, when a herd of elephants arrive.

The highest temperature recorded in Northern Ireland was near Belleek, County Fermanagh, in June 1976 – 87·4° F.

If you double a child's height on their second birthday, it will give you a close estimate as to what their adult height will be. A boy of two is 45.5 per cent of his adult height, and a girl 52.8 per cent of her adult height.

The Queen is forbidden to enter the House of Commons.

A proportion of the air you breathe and the water you drink is not fresh – in the sense that it has already been inhaled or consumed by someone else.

In June 1990 an earthquake in Iran killed forty thousand people. Within six hours the number lost in the tragedy had been replaced by new births worldwide.

Extreme snoring affects 20 per cent of men and 5 per cent of women in the middle-age bracket. A significant medical problem, known as sleep apnoea, occurs when snoring stops and the sufferer fails to breathe momentarily. The brain is deprived of oxygen, which can affect body growth and cause daytime tiredness. In some people sleep apnoea can occur up to nine hundred times a night. In Ireland one-fifth of road accidents are caused by people falling asleep at the wheel.

Henry VII was the only British monarch to be crowned on the battlefield.

Teddy bears are named after the American president, Theodore Roosevelt, who was well known as a hunter of bears.

There is a place in Norway called Hell. There is a town in Sweden called A. Every continent in the world has a city called Rome. There is a village in France called Y.

Mexico once had three different presidents in one day.

In the seventeenth century Englishwomen wore their wedding rings on their thumbs.

From an aeroplane it is possible to see a rainbow as a complete circle.

The former USSR had seven different time zones.

In November 1960 an American rocket launched from Cape Canaveral, Florida, went off course and crashed, killing a cow in Cuba. The Cuban government gave the cow an official funeral as the victim of 'imperial aggression'.

YOU'RE DARN TOOTIN'

Men call women 'birds'
Because of the worms they
pick up.

I don't have a drinking problem.
I drink,
Get drunk,
Fall down.
No problem!

There are only two things in life worth worrying about:
If you are well, or if you are sick.
If you are well, there is nothing to worry about.
And if you are sick, there are only two things to worry about:

If you get better, or if you die.
If you get better, there is nothing to worry about.
And if you die, there are only two things to worry
   about:
If you go to heaven, or if you go to hell.
If you go to heaven, there is nothing to worry about,
And if you go to hell, you are too late to worry.
So why worry?

When I'm right no one remembers.
When I'm wrong no one forgets.

Life begins at forty when things begin to
Fall out,
Spread out and
Wear out.

SON OF THE JOKER

A young and very successful solicitor died. As he stood talking to Saint Peter at the Pearly Gates awaiting his final judgment, he complained to Saint Peter how short his life on earth had been, just thirty-eight years.

'Oh,' said Saint Peter, 'the Lord will be asking for explanations. He had a good reason to take you. He will want to know why, according to the time for which you billed your clients, you are now 104 years old.'

Paddy and Mick had been unemployed for a number of years, but the Government had changed the benefits system so the two boys had to look for work. Paddy went for an interview with an airline company and got the job. Mick then went for an interview with the same company, and when he was asked what he was capable of doing, he told them he was a wood chopper.

'But this is an airline company. We don't have any need for wood choppers,' he was told.

'Paddy got a job here,' complained Mick.

'Yes, but Paddy is a pilot.'

'I know,' said Mick, 'but how can he pile it if I don't chop it first?'

John and Jim set off in their boat for a day's fishing. However, the weather changed and a terrible storm blew up. Night-time came and they were completely at the mercy of the elements.

John started to sob and he prayed. 'Dear God, forgive me for the life I've led. I was constantly drunk, most of my wages I gambled, and when pretty girls were around I soon forgot I was married. But God, if you save my life tonight, I promise faithfully that never again will I drink or –'

'Hold on a minute,' said Jim. 'Don't promise anything more, for I think I see a light.'

A local Romeo took a fancy to a very pretty girl who visited the bar with her friends. He pestered her every time he came across her. Somehow the message that she had no interest in him didn't sink in until one evening when he requested her phone number. She obliged and wrote down the number. That night he dialled the number and the voice at the other end said, 'Hello, Pest Control Limited.'

EAVESDROPPING ON THE PUNTERS

It was a cold and dreary afternoon but the bar was warm and inviting, with the hot whiskeys in great demand.

Jim arrived, and seeing so many customers dressed in their best suits and wearing black ties, he asked, 'Whose funeral was it today?'

'John Flanagan's,' Fergie told him.

'Ah,' said Jim. 'Is he dead? I didn't hear.'

'He'd better be,' said Fergie, 'for they buried him anyhow.'

'I should have been there,' said Jim. 'Was it a big funeral?'

'It was indeed,' said Fergie. 'In the church I was sitting between Billy and Jack. The minister went ranting on about the great man John was, so Billy turned to me and said, "No doubt about it, we're definitely at the wrong funeral." We were tempted to leave but ... well ... we couldn't – seeing about the money an' all.'

'What money?' asked Jim.

'Ach, didn't you know? He wouldn't spend a penny while he was living and when he was dead there were no pockets in the shroud, but sure he must have wanted to take it with him. It seemed a pity, so I wrote a cheque and took his dough. Then we stuck the cheque in with him.'

'Great,' said Jim. 'Right, boys, Fergie here is loaded and wants to buy you all a drink.' Then turning back to Fergie, he said, 'And you never even asked if I had a mouth on me.'

'I didn't need to ask,' said Fergie. 'Sure I can see it swinging between your ears like an old rope.'

Bob, a visitor to the town, called into the bar one night for his pint of good Irish Guinness. The crack was mighty and he was really enjoying himself. He looked up at the clock and noticed it was almost eleven o'clock.

'When does the bar close?' he asked.

'As far as I know,' said Liam, 'it's some time in September.'

Last summer a new slimming club started up in the leisure centre and a craze hit the town. Well, the women took to slimming, while the men proudly displayed their large and extra-large bellies – 'It cost money to put that there.'

One day Jim was telling Tommy how terrific his wife was looking since she had lost so much weight.

Intended as a compliment, Jim said, 'She looks just like a poker.'

'You think so?' asked Tommy. 'Well, let me tell you that a poker sometimes gets nice and warm – unfortunately, never the wife.'

Billy was confiding to his friends that he was thinking of separating from his wife. 'She hasn't spoken to me for six months.'

'Don't be stupid,' advised Mick. 'Think it over, for wives like that are hard to come by.'

Poor Brian's complaint was more difficult. 'I can't work out what makes my wife tick, but I certainly know she can explode.'

On the other hand, Davy felt that he at least had let a little sunshine into his wife's life. 'I arrived home at dawn this morning and as the bedroom door banged, the venetian blind fell down and the sunshine came streaming through.'

Paul reckons that a little consideration goes a long way. He consults his wife before he switches on the TV: 'Do you have anything to say before the football starts?'

The lucky ones come breezing in. 'The wife gave me £2 to have a good night and told me to bring her home the change.'

The pub is often the meeting place for groups of golfers. They play the game on the golf course, then they replay it in the bar. They dissect the game and play it the way they could have done.

Jim was getting a bit of stick one day about his temper. 'I never lose my temper on the golf course,' he retorted. 'It disappears with my first practice swing.'

Jerry's complaint was that before he got married he tried to explain to his wife just how much golf meant to him. 'She has this stupid notion of her own importance. She actually still thinks that she can compete with golf.'

Sammy was telling his mates that he was thinking of putting his house on the market and building a small bungalow for himself and the wife – the house was really much too big for them now. It was a beautiful old house, full of character, but it was supposed to be haunted.

Sammy dismissed this last supposed fact. 'Surely you don't believe in ghosts?'

'Well, I certainly do,' answered Charlie. 'My ex-wife haunts me all the time and she's not even dead yet.'

'Why are you and Teresa always arguing?' Eamon asked Jack.

'Well,' says Jack, 'the only thing we both enjoy are the arguments.'

Eamon, who always had advice for other people, says: 'Maybe you don't try hard enough to be a better husband.'

'Wise up!' says Jack. 'Don't expect me to be better than would be good for me. Sometimes – well, a very odd time – I try to reason with myself, but I'm immediately shot down. I even pray to God to lead me not into temptation but I reckon even he loses the way, for I always head straight into it. Anyway, they talk of miserable sinners but I don't belong to that category. I'm never miserable.'

The education system was under discussion by a group of middle-aged men in the bar one afternoon. With their airs and graces, they no doubt considered themselves superior in knowledge to the young ones.

However, one young lad settled the discussion by saying, 'Don't we all get there one way or another? Ask a statistician what is two plus two and he'll fiddle with his calculator and estimate it to be four. Ask a doctor and he'll suggest four but advise you to get a second opinion. Then ask an accountant and he'll probably ask you what you want it to be. There's room for us all – we've all got a part to play.'

During a holiday period – it was the day after a big night before – a few sore heads came into the bar for a cure.

'I'm never again taking anyone else's advice,' moaned Sam. ' "Give no thought to tomorrow." I followed that yesterday and now ... well, I've got one hell of a hangover.'

'Ay,' says Jim, 'the only thing that will help is a hair of the dog that bit ye. I know if my son decides to follow in my footsteps, I'll not let him live to see the day.'

'Well, put it this way,' says Stephen, 'how would God ever be able to show all His mercy and loving kindness if He hadn't people like you to help Him in His job?'

At this point along came Philip to join the company.

'Well, Philip, what's your great ambition in life?' asked Sam.

'To own a pub,' responded Philip. 'And what's yours?'

'Oh, a double brandy. Thanks, Philip.'

Along the bar sat three women, chatting and laughing together, and Stephen brought them into the conversation.

'Do you ladies have no problems?'

'Like all other wives, the only problems we have are our husbands,' said Jane.

'But Sally isn't even married,' Sam ventured.

'No, that's right,' said Jane. 'She put an ad in the paper looking for a husband and she got hundreds of replies – all from women offering her theirs.'

'Well, maybe some day she'll fall in love,' said Sam.

'Love is the delusion that one man is different from

the rest. The wisest of men can become foolish over women, but the most foolish of women are wise to men.'

'Now, now, you'll have to admit that you have a lot in common with your husbands,' said Philip.

'Yes, we'll admit that,' said Jane. 'We were both married on the same day, at the same time, in the same church, by the same minister.'

'Strange – aren't women strange creatures?'

'Tongues of venom, just like snakes. The only difference is their shape. Now that …'

The men continued to discuss these differences for a while, only to be interrupted with, 'The only difference between men and pigs is that when pigs drink, they don't make men out of themselves.'

A mission was being held in one of the local churches, and inevitably it came up in conversation in the bar. The people attending all seemed very impressed by the missionaries. They reckoned they had gained a lot by it.

John felt that while he was impressed that God had created him out of nothing, he thought it was certainly beginning to show. Also, he says, 'These commandments! I never mean to break them, but somehow, when I'm experimenting, they seem to have no stretch – they just snap.'

'God knows all things,' says Tom. 'Now, I'm a father myself and I know when you tell the children not to do something, it's like putting the idea into their heads. They just can't resist going straight out and doing it. So maybe God just forbids some things so we'll try them out for ourselves.'

'You're right, Tom,' says Fergie. 'If God hadn't provided us with a list of these commandments, sure we're that stupid, half the real interesting ones we'd never have discovered for ourselves.'

Then someone said that, as he came out of church, Kate Mulligan went over to congratulate the missionary on his interesting sermons.

'You really should write them up in a book,' she said, 'so we could read them again and again.'

'Oh, I doubt if they're that good,' replied the missionary. 'And if they are, maybe they'll get published post-humously.'

'Ah, that's great,' said Kate. 'I hope it will be right and soon.'

One afternoon a few men were playing cards in a corner of the bar and some others were playing draughts, but everyone must have been concentrating for there wasn't a lot of chat.

Kevin arrived, ordered a drink, knocked it back, and said, 'Oh, I needed that.'

He told them he had been driving up the road when he saw a man thumbing a lift, so he pulled in for him. He was a gruff character and he had a large bag with him which he threw onto the back seat of the car.

'I told him I was only going a few miles up the road but he asked me if I could take him as far as Belfast,' said Kevin. 'It was essential he got there quickly.

Reluctantly, I agreed. He kept glancing over his shoulder at the bag, so in the end I asked him what was in it. "What's that got to do with you?" he replied. Then I pulled into the side of the road and told him I had to go some place else, so he would have to thumb another lift. He jumped out quickly and ran up the road.'

The men playing cards looked up and Noel asked, 'Did he take his bag?'

'No, he didn't,' answered Kevin.

'And what did you do?' asked Paul.

'I came straight here for a drink.'

'What was in the bag?' queried Noel.

'What's that go to do with you?' retorted Kevin.

The men laughed. 'We walked straight into that,' they said. 'I think we'd better just concentrate on the cards.'

The mood in the bar was sombre one early evening because some of the customers had just heard that the factory where they worked was closing down.

Richard was earwigging a bit and then he started, 'This government –'

Now Richard's views on the Government were heard often, and the same old nonsense repeated over and over again.

To divert this train of conversation, George shouted up to him: 'Richard, do you know the difference between Prince Charles, a bald man, a monkey's mother and an orphan?'

'No, tell us.'

'Well, Prince Charles is the heir apparent, a bald man has no hair apparent, a monkey's mother is a hairy parent and an orphan has ne'er a parent.'

That saved us all from the Government. The

questions and jokes were being thrown back and forth around the bar. George took a piece of paper and wrote something on it. Then he shouted. 'Owen, did you see this one?'

Owen, of course, had to be the person farthest away, and with a bit of bother he made his way up to George to be shown the bit of paper on which was written THIS ONE.

After a few more jokes and puzzles, George again shouted down to Owen. 'Here's a good one.'

And once more Owen pushed his way up the bar to George, this time to be shown a bit of paper on which was written A GOOD ONE. To be caught once was bad enough, but to be caught twice – especially someone like Owen who is usually quick-witted – caused great amusement. Maybe Owen would have preferred to listen to Richard going on about the Government.

In the meantime a young couple due to get married in a few weeks were sitting at the bar, talking to Charlie. Now Charlie believes the only thing to do with good advice is to pass it on to others. He was offering them the name of the very best divorce lawyer in the country. Definitely the very best – the one his ex-wife had had. He also offered Leanne suggestions for keeping her wedding ring bright and new looking – 'Make sure your hands are in the sink or in the wash-hand basin very regularly each day. My ex-wife's ring went very dull because I did too much of the housework.'

Ivor and Davy were about to embark on a new business venture together and were looking for an extra hand. On the notice board in the bar, Ivor put up an ad: WANTED – SMART MEN, BUT NOT TOO SMART. He says he likes people who always speak their minds so then he doesn't make the mistake of employing them.

RETURN OF THE JOKER

This bar was situated opposite a hospital. The bar was packed when the door opened and in came a patient with a drip attached to him. He walks right up to the bar and asks for a double whiskey.

He drinks it straight down and says to the barman, 'I shouldn't be drinking this with what I've got.'

'What have you got?' asks the barman.

'Ten pence,' he answered.

A mouse, being chased by a cat in a public house, fell into a tumbler of whiskey. The mouse begged the cat to get him out and the cat said that he was going to eat him.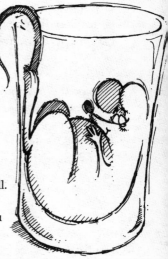

'I don't care about that,' said the mouse. 'I just don't want to die in drink.'

So the cat got the mouse out but the mouse ran into a hole in the wall.

The cat got very cross and said, 'You broke your word. You said you didn't care if I ate you so long as I got you out.'

'Don't be stupid,' says the mouse. 'Who ever listens to what anyone says in drink.'

John was leaning on the bar talking about the most recent tragedy in the town. 'Frank went home early last night and found his wife in bed with the next-door neighbour. He took out his gun and shot the both of them.'

'Well, it could have been worse,' said Jimmy.

'What do you mean – how could anything be worse than that?' said John.

'Well,' said Jimmy, 'if Frank had gone home early the night before I'd be dead by now.'

One Saturday night Davy took his girlfriend down to the pub for a drink. He sat talking about himself non-stop for about an hour – how great he was at golf, the marvellous goalkeeper he was, his views on every subject under the sun. Then he said, 'But that's enough about me – now let's talk about you. What did you think of the way I played in the match last Saturday?'

A motorist drove through a red light.

A policeman stopped him and asked, 'Didn't you see the red light?'

'Yes, I did,' replied the driver.

'Then why didn't you stop?'

'Because I didn't see you.'

In the past penitents, when guilty of serious sin, were given severe penances at confession. Two men who were neighbours were both ordered to make a pilgrimage to a holy well with peas in their boots. They set off together but one man was in agony and just couldn't keep up with the other. He asked him, 'How do you do it? Did you not put the peas in your boots?'

'I did,' replied his neighbour, 'but I boiled them first.'

A man with a giraffe walked into a pub. They drank all afternoon, until around six o'clock, when the giraffe collapsed on the floor. Then his drinking partner staggered towards the door.

'Hey,' said the barman, 'don't leave that lying there.'

The man turned. 'That's not a lion. It's a giraffe.'

Johnny: 'All this nonsense talk about back-seat driving! I've been driving all my life and can safely say I've never heard a word from the back seat.'

Paddy: 'Is that right? What kind of car do you drive?'

Johnny: 'A hearse!'

Two husbands leaning on the bar: 'Did you give your wife a lecture on economy like I told you?' asked one.

'Yes, I certainly did,' replied the other

'And what was the result?'

'I've got to stop smoking.'

Five Hell's Angels walked into the bar and ordered a round of drinks, saying that a man sitting alone along the bar was paying. When the man refused, they punched him and threw him onto the street.

'He wasn't much of a fighter,' said one of the bikers to the barman.

'He's not much of a driver either,' said the barman. 'He's just had an accident and driven over five motorbikes.'

Johnny was up in court.

'Your Honour, I wasn't intoxicated,' he explained, 'I simply had a bit to drink.'

'Oh, I see,' the judge replied. 'In that case, I sentence you to thirty days in prison instead of one month.'

During a quarrel a wife said to her husband, 'You know, I was a fool when I married you.'

Her husband replied, 'Yes dear, but I was in love then and I didn't notice it.'

Nothing much was happening in the afterworld one day, so the devil challenged Saint Peter to a football match.

'Remember,' says Saint Peter, 'we have all the good footballers up here.'

'Ah, I know,' says the devil, 'but we've got all the referees and umpires down here.'

Johnny was going off on holidays so he went to the barber's to get a good haircut first.

'Be sure you come round and tell me all about it when you get back,' said the barber.

About six weeks later the man went back to the barber's and told him all about the holiday.

'… then we went to Rome. I even had a private audience with the pope.'

'My goodness! And what did HE have to say?' asked the barber.

'He asked me where in hell I got my hair cut.'

EXTRA BAFFLERS

Answers on page 90

1 What is at the end of life and at the beginning of eternity?

2 Give the following to a friend to read aloud:

    Si Señor, dere dego,
    Forte lorez inaroe.
    Demaint lorez, demis trux,
    Fulou ensean geesan dux.

3 Claire was nine the day before yesterday. Next year she will be twelve. How could this be possible?

4 YYURYYUBICURYY4ME – translate.

5 MNXRLT4U – translate.

6 What is it that everybody accepts is between heaven and earth?

PULL THE OTHER ONE!

Jane loved children and often babysat for friends. One night she was looking after three children who lived out of town in a beautiful old house, up a tree-lined avenue. The parents had gone out for a meal and the children were playing in the lounge with Jane, having been allowed to stay up later than usual.

The phone rang and when Jane answered it, all she could hear was heavy breathing. She hung up, but immediately it rang again and this time the caller told her that he knew exactly where she was. By now Jane was extremely worried and when a third call threatened murder, she phoned the police. They told her that if he called again, to keep him talking for as long as possible and they would put a trace on the call. A little later the phone rang again; it was the same caller so she kept him talking for as long as she could. No sooner had she hung up, than two cars came screaming up the avenue. She was really scared until she saw it was the police.

'Get out of here immediately and take the children with you – into the second police car – quick,' shouted an officer. 'We traced the call and it's the other line in the house. The nutter is in the house with you.'

An old man in the bar told a story about himself as a young lad, when he and his mates used to play a trick on the ducks in the park.

They would go to the lake, take a length of string and tie a piece of fatty bacon rind to it. The hungry ducks would swim over to them to get their treat. The lads would throw the bacon rind to the first duck who would gobble it up immediately.

Now maybe you don't know this, but bacon rind goes through a duck like a dose of salts. So, the bacon rind went through the first duck and floated on the water until a second duck came along and swallowed it up. The same thing continued until all the ducks were in a straight line, connected to each other by the length of string.

The lads would then play and laugh at the ducks and eventually take one duck and pull its leg – just as I'm pulling yours.

Billy came into the bar one afternoon with a dour look on his face.

'Did you enjoy yourself last night?' he was asked by one of his mates who had been at the same stag party as Billy the previous night.

'I enjoyed the party but not the follow-up,' said Billy.

'Why, what happened? The old lady cross?' asked John.

'No, she doesn't know yet,' said Billy. 'I was driving home real careful, but as I turned into Bridge Street I crashed into a BMW parked with no lights on outside Rodney's. There was nobody around so I reversed and sped away as fast as I could. As soon as I got home I lay on the couch and fell fast asleep.'

'Did you damage the car badly?' asked John.

'Well, about ten minutes after I got home the police arrived and accused me of drunk driving and crashing into a BMW. I hadn't a clue who could have seen me and wondered if the police station camera might have picked it up, but then the policeman produced the number plate of my car.'

'You left it embedded in the back of the BMW,' he said.

One Sunday afternoon Nigel and Tom decided to take a trip to the seaside. It was a lovely afternoon and the car park was packed, but eventually they found a convenient parking spot on the seafront. They spent a very pleasant afternoon in the town and were on their way back to the car when they saw Jim, a neighbour from home who was rather fond of the bottle, lying drunk on the footpath being a nuisance to passers-by and a danger to himself. They stopped and gathered him up but couldn't get any sense out of him, so they laid him on the back seat of the car and drove him home.

By the time they reached home Jim still hadn't sobered up, so Nigel searched Jim's pockets and found his door key. He unlocked the door and they carried Jim into the house and laid him on the living room couch, thinking he would sleep it off.

Next day, as Nigel was driving down the street, he saw Jim standing at the bus stop. He puzzled at this as Jim usually travelled by car, so he stopped to talk to him.

'I don't know how it happened,' said Jim, 'but for the first time in my life I took the wife and children to the seaside for a holiday but I woke up this morning on the couch at home.'

Tim was a real big-timer. One night he had been in the city, living it up at a champagne party, and in the early hours he got into his Porsche and set off for home up the M1. He was speeding for all he was worth and thinking so much about some pretty girls at the party that he missed his turn on the motorway. He didn't want to drive to the next turn-off and add miles to his journey, so he screeched to a halt, and as there was no sign of anything behind him, he decided to chance reversing to his turning in the outside lane.

He slammed the car into reverse, pressed hard on the accelerator and careered backwards. BANG! An old jigger drove right into him. The police arrived on the scene very quickly and Tim felt himself sobering up as he thought of the trouble he'd be in. He'd lose his licence for a year – how would he manage?

'Excuse me, sir,' said a policeman at the window of his car, 'are you all right?'

Tim was shaking his head. The policeman leaned down and said: 'This man in the car behind is blocked out of his mind. He actually thinks you were reversing in the fast lane.'

Mary called into the bar one afternoon for a beer. She worked as a home help and was very conscientious in her work. In fact, she looked after the elderly people as if they were her own parents.

One old man who lived alone was not feeling well, so Mary had called to see him in the afternoon to check on how he was and to chat to him for a while. He was delighted to see her and wanted to make her welcome so he offered her a bag of peanuts. To please him, she ate some of the nuts but he pressed her to eat them all.

As she munched her way through them he told her, 'I can't eat peanuts, anyhow. They stick in the few teeth I have left so I just suck the chocolate off them.'

One evening Stephen surprised Claire by inviting her for a meal at a newly opened Chinese restaurant. They took Claire's pride and joy, her little dog, with them.

During the meal the dog started to whine so Claire called one of the waiters over and asked him if he could bring something for her little dog to keep him happy and not feel left out. The waiter didn't understand her. He just shook his head and grunted. She then tried to explain using sign language, pointing to the dog and to her plate, saying, 'yum, yum'.

The waiter then indicated that he understood, so he took the dog by the lead and led it away from the table. Now both of them were home birds who rarely dined out and they were really enjoying their meal when, about twenty minutes later, the waiter returned with more food. To their horror it was the little dog, roasted and served on a silver platter and garnished with tomato, cucumber and orange slices in its mouth.

Roy is a real gentleman who earns his money as a long distance lorry driver. He came into the bar one night to steady his nerves. He'd been on a long run and the weather was atrocious, teeming out of the heavens all day, conditions which can make driving a very tiring occupation. As he drove along, with his wipers going full blast and his headlights on, he suddenly saw a cat sitting on the road in front of him. He slammed on the brakes. The lorry skidded and there was a horrible bump.

Now Roy is a kind man and is actually a cat lover, so it upset him to see the stricken cat on the verge. He did what he considered to be the decent thing: he took a shovel to the cat and put it out of its agony.

There was a nasty twist to the story when an old lady phoned the police to report Roy for running over her next door neighbour's cat and then stopping the lorry and using a shovel to kill *her* beloved cat.

THE THINGS YOU HEAR

It was lunch time and in the bar a group of five men sat drinking their pints. Gavin, a local reporter, was telling the others about the barbecue at the local rugby club the previous night.

'A brilliant night's crack but it wasn't so good this morning. I had to interview old Sarah Miles – she's ninety-nine, you know. When I was leaving I told her I hoped I'd interview her next year for her one hundredth birthday but she said she doubted it. She wasn't thinking of herself but decided that going by the way I looked I mightn't make it till next year. Talk about cheek!'

Tony was leaving his job and Henry asked him if his boss was surprised.

'Not at all,' said Tony. 'He knew all about it before I did.' He had gone for an interview that afternoon and was told the pay would be £280 a week if the work was satisfactory. 'Ah,' said Tony, 'I just knew there would be a catch in it somewhere.'

Harry had been in his job for a long number of years – in fact, ever since he left school. He never missed a day if he could possibly help it.

'Why are you always so anxious to go to work?' asked Gavin. 'Do you think the firm can't get along without you?'

'You couldn't be further from the truth,' said Harry. 'I'm just worried that if I'm not there, they might realise that they can.'

As they chatted they were watching another man further up along the bar. He was a regular customer, a middle-aged man, who always enjoyed his wee drink but on this day, as he drank, he repeatedly closed his eyes. The group of men reckoned there was definitely something amiss with him. Eventually Harry asked him what was wrong.

In a sad voice the man told him: 'I promised the wife I would never look at another drink again.'

THE JOKER RIDES AGAIN

An attractive young woman was sitting alone in a bar when a young man approached her.

'May I buy you a drink?' he asked.

'What! To a motel?' she screamed.

'No, no!' protested the man. 'You misunderstood – I just asked if you would like a drink.'

'You are asking me to go to a motel,' she yelled even louder.

Completely bewildered, the young man retreated to a corner table and everyone in the bar glared at him indignantly.

After ten minutes the young woman came over to him to explain. 'I'm a psychology student studying human behaviour in unexpected situations.'

The young man looked at her and shouted, 'What? You want £100!'

She prided herself as the perfect model of Christianity and judged all and everyone in the village as below par. One day she rebuked a workman for drinking. 'I saw your car parked outside the pub all yesterday afternoon,' she said.

The accused made no defence but that night he parked his car outside her house and left it till morning.

Two businessmen, during their lunch break, set off to the local club to play a round of golf. Two women playing ahead of them were slowing the men's game down.

Jack said, 'I'll go and ask them would they mind if we play through.'

He hadn't got as far as the women when he turned and hurried back. 'Sam, you won't believe this, but one is my wife and the other is my mistress.'

'Not to worry, Jack, I'll approach them and you keep your head down while we play past them.'

Sam had only gone a hundred yards when he rushed back. 'You're not going to believe this, Jack, but one is my wife and the other is my mistress too.'

Billy arrived home very late from the pub – well-oiled and ready for trouble.

As he stumbled up the stairs his wife called out, 'Is that you, Billy?'

'By God, it had damned well better be,' said Billy.

'Do you think I'm conceited?' a young hotshot asked his girlfriend.

'No. Why do you ask?'

'Well, when I was a baby I won a bonny baby competition and usually anyone who's as handsome as I am is conceited.'

The minister was delivering a very fine sermon on the evils of alcohol. 'I've lived in this town now for twenty years and I can truly say that although there are ten pubs I have never been in one of them.'

'Which one of them was that?' shouted a voice from the congregation.

A man went to confession and explained that he had stolen a bit of old rope.

'Oh, I wouldn't think that was very serious,' said the priest. 'I wouldn't worry too much about that.'

'But,' the man said, 'there was a pig on the end of it.'

The landlord, out early one bright spring morning, came across a poacher.

'You are out very early this morning, sir,' said the poacher.

'I like to get an appetite for my breakfast,' replied the landlord, and added, 'what brought you out so early?'

'To get a breakfast for my appetite,' rejoined the poacher.

A publican, who had been in the trade a very long time, died and went up to the Pearly Gates.

Saint Peter came to meet him. 'You've had a long time on earth. How did you spend your time?' he asked.

'Unfortunately,' said the publican, 'most of it was spent on the wrong side of the bar. You see, I was a publican.'

'Oh dear,' said Saint Peter, 'you have really had your hell on earth. Now it's your turn. Would you like to come in and have a Harp.'

It was 3.00 a.m. and a worried husband paced up and down the bedroom floor.

'What's wrong with you?' said his wife, who couldn't sleep with his pacing.

'I'm sick with worry. There's an electric bill, a phone bill, the rates are due and so is the mortgage and no matter how hard I work I just can't seem to get on top. If I write a cheque there's no money in the bank to cover it.'

The wife got out of bed and made a phone call. Then she

called her husband to bed.

'I've settled it,' she said, 'I told the bank manager he wouldn't be getting any money from you. We'll keep our overdraft the way it is. That's what he's paid a fat salary for, so he can pace his room for the rest of the night. No point the two of you worrying.'

In ancient Rome a Christian was being pursued by a lion. He ran out into the woods and dodged through the trees. It soon became obvious that he had no chance of escaping, so he turned to the lion and fell to his knees.

'Lord,' he prayed desperately, 'make this lion a Christian.'

The lion then dropped to its knees and prayed. 'For what we are about to receive, Lord, make us truly thankful.'

A man caught a boy stealing apples in an orchard. He grabbed the boy by the arm and said he was taking him to the farmer for punishment. On the way, the boy remembered he'd left his cap behind.

'All right,' said the man. 'I'll wait here while you go back to get it.'

The boy never returned.

The following week he caught the boy in the orchard again. 'This time you're going to be punished if I have to drag you all the way to the farmer.'

Before they reached the farm the boy announced that he'd left his cap behind in the orchard.

The man laughed scornfully. 'You don't catch me twice the same way, boy. You wait here and I'll go back and get it.'

Seated beside a grumpy old fellow in the bar one day, a cheerful young man tried to open a conversation.

'Do you like fishing, sir?'

'No. Tried it once. Didn't like it,' was the reply.

Later the young man tried again. 'Ever go to the cinema?'

'No. Tried it once. Didn't like it,' again came the reply, but this time he added, 'You look about the same age as my son.'

'Your only family, sir?' enquired the young man.

There was a fortune-teller at the local fair day and, to please his wife, John paid her a visit. He was very sceptical but sat down in front of the crystal ball.

'I see you're the father of two children,' she began.

'Ha, you don't know everything. I'm the father of three children.'

'Ha, *you* don't know everything,' smiled the fortune-teller.

DID YOU EVER HEAR
THE LIKE OF THAT?

Pat was a bus driver for many years. There is one incident that he'll always remember and he relates it regularly to his friends.

One evening, when he finished his run for the day, he brought the bus back to the garage and, as always, took a look around to check that nothing was out of place. On one seat he found a little wooden box, beautifully carved, and when he opened it he found it was full of suspicious-looking powder. He brought it to the office where his manager, a very efficient and bossy man, dipped his finger in and tasted it.

'It's narcotics,' said Mr Know-All.

Just then a feeble old lady walked into the office to enquire if they'd found a small casket containing her husband's ashes.

Robert was getting married and contrary to his fiancées wishes he chose as his best man a rather uncouth fellow rugby player, who was always boasting and loved to belittle others.

However, on the day of the wedding his behaviour was impeccable. He conducted himself in an admirable way and at the end of the night he waved the newly-weds off on their honeymoon.

They spent a wonderful night in the honeymoon suite of a luxurious hotel. In the morning they awoke late and immediately started into a passionate sequel to the night before. Afterwards the groom rang up room service and requested breakfast in bed for two.

'Make that three,' shouted the best man from beneath the bed.

A glamorous, middle-aged lady who comes into the bar with her wealthy old husband is the subject of a story other customers tell about the early sixties.

The beehive was a very hip hairstyle at that time and this same lady was then a fashionable young woman. All the girls backcombed their hair to make it sit up as high as possible and then they smoothed it over and applied hairspray to keep it in place. The more spray you used, the better the beehive. Of course, washing it always ruined the effect but somehow this girl's beehive was never anything short of perfect and many wondered how she managed it. Then one day it became all too clear why she never had a hair out of place – for weeks on end she had not combed it out and had just applied more spray each day. She was taken to hospital and her hair was shaved off. Apparently, beetles were nesting inside her beehive.

Some residents of Beech Road were not too happy when a new family moved into the estate. They were the all-night-party type – lots of noise and a nuisance. They also had an untrained, hyperactive dog that messed up the gardens, carried things from the back yard, and even pulled clothes off the line.

One day the mongrel arrived home with a white rabbit in its mouth. The dog's owner reckoned this would be the last straw. They'd never be welcomed in the estate now, especially as he knew the rabbit belonged to the children next door. Luckily, the dog hadn't chewed the rabbit – it was just dirty and dead. This gave him an idea. He took the rabbit, carefully shampooed and blow-dried it, and then, when he knew the family next door had all gone out, he hopped over the fence and placed the rabbit in its hutch.

Next day he was out in his garden drinking a can of lager when he saw his next-door neighbour. Hoping to become accepted by the neighbours, he spoke to her about the lovely day it was. She told him her children were very upset.

'It's about the rabbit,' she said.

He felt very uncomfortable but enquired what had happened to the rabbit.

'It died two days ago and we buried it yesterday but last night it was back in its hutch again,' she said.

QUIZMASTER

NAME THESE TOWNS AND VILLAGES IN NORTHERN IRELAND

Answers on page 91

1 Prohibit the card game
2 Paid to dance
3 Rapid ringing
4 On the edge of insect walks
5 After the nails are mixed, he's off for his winter sport
6 Factories situated on a biblical mount
7 Trifling leave
8 Chef's home
9 Wan music
10 Angry mother's dell
11 Is going into law with ringing device
12 Dead beam
13 A jumbled rail within him
14 A mother shared
15 Isn't she tall both front and back
16 Trinity's famous book
17 Society dance in a duck
18 Speedy wine
19 Or knife valley
20 Sacred forest
21 Crossing point after piece of fish
22 Sheltered dale with Royal face
23 The sword partly follows the girl
24 Cosmetics salesman

NAME THESE TOWNS AND BOROUGHS IN GREAT BRITAIN

Answers on page 91

1 Thump the craftsman
2 Finished digging that hole
3 A letter below the earth
4 Dark fire

5 Colours the town
6 Safe place for a wedding
7 He covers a wheel
8 Fresh from the boats
9 Carry on tearing
10 Electric control added on
11 This small boy is there
12 In aid of a long distance
13 Top of the entrance
14 You could swim in all this water
15 Dee is finished now
16 A short maiden's hair replacement

NAME THESE COUNTRIES
Answers on page 91

1 Not a full aspirin
2 Fishy, but not at sea
3 Utensil mother uses
4 FN gets lost in the race
5 Added enthusiasm that isn't old
6 Might the boy be after a hideaway
7 Queue if you're not in a hurry
8 It's not a journey south
9 Lubricant
10 It's serious when entering the brain

NAME THESE BIRDS
Answers on page 91

1 The lady with the lamp
2 Speedy
3 Won't steal outside
4 Could not be seen at night
5 The monarch of the anglers
6 Grumble
7 This girl is a good cook
8 Could it be a happy dog?
9 A hundred goes before an argument
10 R is not old but very mixed up

NAME THESE RIVERS IN THE BRITISH ISLES

Answers on page 91

1 Reversed, this won't say no to a short remembrance
2 A tasty morsel of meat after a cuppa isn't enough
3 Plenty in the golf bag
4 This fellow needs the revenue
5 Confused and abbreviated – NEVER
6 S goes first as it won't ever happen because of the confusion
7 To forbid it isn't quite enough
8 Sheltered
9 Sounds as though it has a gentle flow
10 The French horse goes backwards.

NAME THESE CITIES AND TOWNS IN IRELAND

Answers on page 91

1 It wouldn't require a complete cutting
2 Nearly murdered in a hurry
3 A donkey might feel at home here
4 A brand of shoe to wear on a deformed foot
5 A slang convict backwards has his own route
6 A magnificent building that can't be new
7 A water fowl's climb
8 The perfect bid for a bottle of wine
9 Might your kith be sold cheap?
10 Forbid the effort
11 Certainly not a short crossing
12 Why is the lamp not shining?
13 What sort of mixed-up animal might this be?
14 Not only a house of prayer
15 Noah landed but not on Mount Avarat
16 A gateway opposite the eastern entrance
17 A fruit mixed with CL
18 The spectators might not see the _____ scrum
19 A pretty dell
20 An unusual substance for an incline

NAME THESE TREES
Answers on page 92

1 A very old fruit
2 Flick away
3 It's fun to play here
4 Animal jigsaw
5 Type of syrup
6 Sounds like he's ill again
7 Won't make a gold cane
8 This man won't climb heights
9 For the animal to crack or roast
10 Mel gets somewhat confused

NAME THESE FLOWERS
Answers on page 92

1 Lady has no free time
2 Always remembered
3 Sign of winter when not so
4 She's up in the mountains
5 He's got two eyes, two ears and …
6 Not a bitter accompaniment to fish and chips
7 Wed with a ring not silver
8 First sign of winter
9 It makes the city proud
10 Part of your eye
11 Are the people all on wheels?
12 This animal may fall
13 This animal goes boxing

NAME THESE SWEET SENSATIONS
Answers on page 92

1 Wobbly infants
2 Variety of liquorice
3 Sounds like the snow is coming
4 Whisper softly
5 Sport fit for a prince
6 Dabble in the occult
7 Edible fasteners
8 Allows for stargazers
9 Precious metal
10 Fruit is falling

11 Flower bouquet
12 Can carry the dairy produce
13 The cats just love it
14 Wise guys

NAME THESE PREMIERSHIP FOOTBALLERS
Answers on page 92

1   This D is the Grand Old Duke
2   This T brightens up your home either inside or out
3   This I uses his mitre to ooze authority
4   This D is the fifth of twelve
5   This S sounds like a shaggy dog with a little bit extra
6   This R is a sly old boy
7   This D is a drink with a Spanish hello
8   This N finds no one up north
9   This C shows his hand with the casualty department
10 This D is the fair city
11 This K may hear a ring while he's in his tent
12 This I has life in its corridor
13 This M is like an early morning fruit
14 This D is dark, deep and wet
15 This C has a trade no longer required
16 This C is a limb but no weakling
17 This D is a vegetable with a chicken
18 This G is an entrance opposite the north
19 This D doesn't make his living on the land
20 This D doesn't lack common sense

A QUESTION OF SPORT
Answers on page 92

1   Are they mints or sportsmen?
2   This champion horse was murder
3   Would you play, crush or squeeze this fruity sport?
4   Did Buddy Holly like this game?
5   This darts player sounds more interested in horses
6   Is whiskey made in the Irish league?
7   A hurricane over a game of snooker
8   A tooth used for fencing
9   My father's brother's son won a 1980 Olympic gold medal
10 It's not round or square but good for cricket

ANSWERS

BAFFLED AND BEWILDERED
Questions on page 14

1
```
        888
         88
          8
          8
    +     8
    ─────────
      1,000
```

2 Because of the repetition, many will say GIGFU instead of GIGFY.

3 Turn the Hennessy bottle upside down; there's an indent in the bottom of the bottle which will hold a halfun. Fill a halfun into it and drink.

4 10 T0 10; stroke over the second 1 to make it ten to ten, which is 9.50.

5 The cost of the room was £25 or £27 minus £2. The mistake arises from adding £27 to £2 and getting the misleading figure of £29.

6

7 1 0 2 0 0 4 1 8 0
I ought to owe nothing for I ate nothing.

8 Place a linen cloth over your forefinger and slowly pour the whiskey through the cloth and it will sit on top of the water without mixing.

9 He was wearing his uniform. Invariably the person asked the question takes the piece of paper and studies it, looking for a clue.

10 35

11

12

| T | E | N | H | O | R | S | E | S |

13 545 + 5 = 550
Use a stroke to make the first + sign a 4.

14

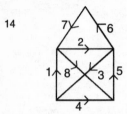

15 T – they are all the letters adjacent to the vowels
16 5 boys and 11 girls
17 The man was a dwarf and could only reach up to the third
button.

18

19 Water – it's the letters from H to O (H_2O).

20

| A | B | C | D | E | F | | First set up the glasses like this |

Move A and B to the far right

| | | C | D | E | F | A | B | |

Move F and A to the far right

| A | D | D | | | B | F | A | |

Lastly move C and D between E and B

| | | E | C | D | B | F | A | |

21 N and T – OTTFFSSE are the initial letters of words One, Two,
Three, Four, Five, Six, Seven, Eight; N is the initial letter of
nine, T the initial letter of ten.
22 Wind a £5 note tightly round the cigarette and you can then
gently join top and bottom without breaking it.

23

24 6 to first
   3 to second
   2 to third.
   (But 6 isn't half of 11)
   He got his neighbour to lend him 1 cow. Then he divided them
   exactly 6 − 3 − 2 and then returned his neighbour's cow.

25 Scrambled eggs

26 £99.98

27 $1 + 1 + 1 = 3$
   $2 \div 2 + 2 = 3$
   $3 - 3 + 3 = 3$
   $4 - (4 \div 4) = 3$
   $0.5 + (5 \times 0.5) = 3$
   $(6 \times 0.6) - 0.6 = 3$
   $(7 \div 0.7) - 7 = 3$
   $\sqrt{(8 \div 8)} + 8 = 3$
   $\sqrt{9} - 9 + 9 = 3$

28   15
          36
          47
        + 2
        ─────
         100

29 Take a gent's handkerchief and constantly twisting it bring it to
   the bottom of the bottle anchoring the cork. Slowly ease it up
   until near the top. Then pull as though opening a wine bottle. It
   will come out with a pop.

30 Answer as illustrated in question, p.17

31 Twenty-four triangles

32 Press your thumb tightly over the top of the bottle and hold it
   there. Eventually the matchstick tops will sink one at a time. Lift
   your thumb when the second one reaches the middle. (The first
   will already be at the bottom and the third still at the top.)

33 At the 800-mile point it flew over the North Pole.

34 The man takes the hen across first. Then he goes back and
   takes the fox across, but as he cannot leave the fox and the

hen together he brings the hen back. Then he takes the corn across and goes back and collects the hen.

35 Initially he can make 38 candles + 3 stubs. Burning 38 candles, he will have enough stubs for 4 new candles + 2 stubs (now leaving him with 5 stubs). Burning the 4 new candles, he will now have 4 stubs + 2 stubs + 3 stubs, enough for 1 new candle. Altogether: 38 + 4 + 1 = 43 candles.

36 Put a piece of match, containing the head, into the butt of a cigarette and float it like a canoe in the water. Light the match head and then place the glass on top. The match will go out and the water will rise into the glass.

37 Fold over a corner of a sheet of paper and at the point of the folded corner place a dot on the sheet. Without lifting your pen draw a line from the dot onto the folded corner and continue to the edge of the folded corner and then onto the sheet. Now lift up the fold and complete the circle.

38

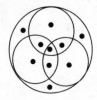

39 Attack at dawn Monday (first letter of each word).

40 Pour milk from bucket number 2 into bucket number 5.

41 Pour four of the half full barrels together to make two full barrels and two empty barrels. Now there are nine full, three half full and nine empty barrels. Divide by three and each son gets three full barrels, one half full and three empty barrels.

42

43   5 of Toy A
      1 of Toy B
      94 of Toy C

44 He could get a box 3ft by 4ft and place the fishing rod
   diagonally inside.

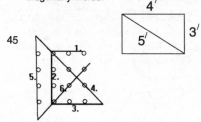

45

46 Refrigerator
47 Twenty
48

49 His son

THINK TANK

Questions on page 39

1 The perfect woman – Santa Claus doesn't exist and neither
   does the perfect man.
2 A man who never Mrs anyone.
3 Look at it through a magnifying glass.
4 Jimmy Never played with Bolton and he scored.
5 Celtic – the turf for its pitch was taken from Ballykinler, County
   Down.
6 The match
7 No – only dead people are buried.
8 No – to have a widow he must be dead and dead men don't
   marry.
9 Yes – but it's not a holiday.
10 You are the captain – your age.
11 Day 59
12 They both played with other people.
13 House numbers
14 He says: 'I will be shot.'
15 Lay an egg the same colour as itself.
16 QUEUE

17 You don't bury survivors.

18 None – it was Noah who had the ark.

19 All of them. Some, of course, have more than 28 days.

20 S Strachan
   C Cooper
   O O'Hare
   T Templeton
   L Law
   A Archibald
   N Nevin
   D Dalglish

21 Electric trains do not have smoke.

22

23 INDIVISIBILITY

24 EERIE

25 LATCHSTRING

26 FACETIOUSLY or ABSTEMIOUSLY

27 Since one of them will be (x – x), which is zero, the answer is zero.

EXTRA BAFFLERS

Questions on page 64

1 The letter E

2 Inevitably they put on their best Spanish accent – but it actually reads:

   > Si Señor, there they go,
   > Forty lorries in a row,
   > Them ain't lorries, them is trucks,
   > Full of hens and geese and ducks.

3 Today is 1 January; Claire's birthday was yesterday, 31 December. Therefore she was nine on 30 December, ten on 31 December, she'll be eleven at the end of the year, and so will be twelve next year.

4 Too wise you are, too wise you be. I see you are too wise for me.

5 Ham and eggs are healthy for you.

6 The word 'and'

TOWNS AND VILLAGES IN NORTHERN IRELAND

Questions on page 80

1 Banbridge
2 Ballymoney
3 Belfast
4 Antrim
5 Lisnaskea
6 Sion Mills
7 Pettigo
8 Cookstown
9 Tempo
10 Crossmaglen
11 Lisbellaw
12 Kilrea
13 Maralin
14 Armagh
15 Annalong
16 Kells
17 Ballinamallard
18 Portrush
19 Forkhill
20 Holywood
21 Gilford
22 Glenavy
23 Annahilt
24 Craigavon

TOWNS AND BOROUGHS IN GREAT BRITAIN

Questions on page 80

1 Hammersmith
2 Gravesend
3 Sunderland
4 Blackburn
5 Staines
6 Whitehaven
7 Doncaster
8 Newquay
9 Ripon
10 Ipswich
11 Edinburgh
12 Forfar
13 Gateshead
14 Poole
15 Dundee
16 Wigan

COUNTRIES

Questions on page 81

1 Spain
2 Finland
3 Panama
4 France
5 New Zealand
6 Denmark
7 Kuwait
8 Norway
9 Greece
10 Great Britain

BIRDS

Questions on page 81

1 Nightingale
2 Swift
3 Robin
4 Blackbird
5 Kingfisher
6 Grouse
7 Magpie
8 Wagtail
9 Crow
10 Wren

RIVERS IN THE BRITISH ISLES

Questions on page 82

1 Mersey
2 Thames
3 Tees
4 Trent
5 Erne
6 Severn
7 Bann
8 Lee
9 Ouse
10 Lagan

CITIES AND TOWNS IN IRELAND

Questions on page 82

1 Trim
2 Kilrush
3 Bray
4 Ballybunion
5 Galway
6 Oldcastle
7 Cootehill

8 Cork
9 Kinsale
10 Bantry
11 Longford
12 Wicklow
13 Ardee
14 Templemore
15 Arklow
16 Westport
17 Clonmel
18 Ballina
19 Dingle
20 Salthill

TREES
Questions on page 83

1 Elderberry
2 Ash
3 Beech
4 Monkey puzzle
5 Maple
6 Sycamore
7 Silver birch
8 Willow
9 Horse chestnut
10 Elm

FLOWERS
Questions on page 83

1 Busy Lizzie
2 Forget-me-not
3 Snow-in-summer
4 Heather
5 Tulips
6 Sweet pea
7 Marigold
8 Snowdrop
9 London pride
10 Iris
11 Carnation
12 Cowslip
13 Foxglove

SWEET SENSATIONS
Questions on page 83

1 Jelly Babies
2 Allsorts
3 Flake
4 Wispa
5 Polo
6 Black Magic

7 Chocolate Buttons
8 Galaxy
9 All Gold
10 Pear drops
11 Roses
12 Milk Tray
13 Kit Kat
14 Smarties

PREMIERSHIP FOOTBALLERS
Questions on page 84

1 Dwight Yorke
2 Tim Flowers
3 Ian Bishop
4 David May
5 Stan Collymore
6 Ruel Fox
7 David Ginola
8 Neville Southall
9 Carlton Palmer
10 Dion Dublin
11 Kevin Campbell
12 Ian Marshall
13 Michael Duberry
14 Dean Blackwell
15 Colin Cooper
16 Chris Armstrong
17 Darren Peacock
18 Gareth Southgate
19 David Seaman
20 Dennis Wise

A QUESTION OF SPORT
Questions on page 84

1 Everton
2 Red Rum
3 Squash
4 Cricket
5 Jockey Wilson
6 Distillery
7 Alex Higgins
8 Sabre
9 Robin Cousins
10 The Oval